MW01641258

Gratitude

Journal

Keeping a Gratitude Journal for Kids

A gratitude journal is a great way to keep yourself in a thankful and positive state of mind. Here are some tips on what to write in and how to keep your gratitude journal going.

1. Think about the people in your life that you are grateful for like your parents, grandparents, sisters and brothers, teachers and friends.
2. Consider things and experiences you have been through and why you are grateful you are able to have them.
3. How was your day today? Write down what you are thankful for today.
4. Consider your abilities and skills and why you are thankful for them. Did you pass your math test? Did you get a good grade in school?

5. Consider capturing moments and taping pictures to a page for those days you do not have words.
6. Try to write often a few things you are grateful for but try not to repeat yourself all the time because that will make writing in your gratitude journal more challenging on a daily or weekly basis.
7. Make a schedule but allow yourself to skip days if needed. Do you want to write daily? Weekly?
8. Don't feel like writing? Use the blank pages to draw what you are grateful for or paste a photo to the page if you like.

Today I am grateful for

Today I am grateful for

Today I am grateful for

Today I am grateful for

Today I am grateful for

Today I am grateful for

Today I am grateful for

Today I am grateful for

Today I am grateful for

Today I am grateful for

Today I am grateful for

____

____

____

____

____

____

Today I am grateful for

Today I am grateful for

Today I am grateful for

Today I am grateful for

Today I am grateful for

Today I am grateful for

Today I am grateful for

Today I am grateful for

Today I am grateful for

Today I am grateful for

Today I am grateful for

Today I am grateful for

Today I am grateful for

Today I am grateful for

Today I am grateful for

Today I am grateful for

____

____

____

____

____

____

Today I am grateful for

Today I am grateful for

Today I am grateful for

Today I am grateful for

Today I am grateful for

Today I am grateful for

____

____

____

____

____

____

Today I am grateful for

Today I am grateful for

Today I am grateful for

Today I am grateful for

____

____

____

____

____

____

Today I am grateful for

Today I am grateful for

Today I am grateful for

Today I am grateful for

Today I am grateful for

Today I am grateful for

Today I am grateful for

Today I am grateful for

Made in the USA
Middletown, DE
17 September 2017